DK Eye Wonder
Space

LONDON, NEW YORK, MUNICH,
MELBOURNE, DELHI

Written and edited by Simon Holland
Designed by Tanya Tween, Claire Penny,
and Tory Gordon-Harris

Publishing manager Mary Ling
Managing art editor Rachael Foster
US editors Gary Werner and Margaret Parrish
Jacket design Chris Drew
Picture researcher Jo Haddon
Production Kate Oliver
DTP designer Almudena Díaz
Space consultant Carole Stott

First American Edition, 2001
10 11 12 15 14 13

Published in the United States by
DK Publishing, Inc.
375 Hudson Street
New York, New York 10014

Copyright © 2001 Dorling Kindersley Limited

Library of Congress Cataloging-in-Publication Data
Holland, Simon, 1955–
    Space / by Simon Holland.— 1st American ed.
        p. cm. -- (Eye Wonder)
    Includes index.
    ISBN 0-7894-7854-4 -- ISBN 0-7894-8182-0 (lib. bdg.)
    1. Astronomy--Juvenile literature.
    [1. Outer Space. 2. Astronomy.] I. Title. II. Series.
    QB46 .H73 2001
    520--dc21   2001017277
        ISBN-13 978-0-7894-7854-2

Color reproduction by Colourscan, Singapore
Printed and bound in Italy by L.E.G.O.

See our complete
catalog at
www.dk.com

Contents

4-5
Staring into space

6-7
Our place in space

8-9
A closer look

10-11
Journey to the Moon

12-13
Earth's moon

14-15
The Sun

16-17
Family of the Sun

18-19
Mercury and friends

20-21
Sister Venus

22-23
The Red Planet

24-25
A rocky racetrack

26-27
King of the planets

28-29
Planet of the rings

30-31
Distant twins

32-33
Pluto and the comets

34-35
Secrets of the stars

36-37
The Milky Way

38-39
About the universe

40-41
Liftoff

42-43
Life in space

44-45
Our future in space

46-47
Space glossary

48
Index and
acknowledgments

Staring into space

Staring into space is something people do all the time. On a clear night, we are able to see bright objects in the sky. These objects are in space. Things in space look like tiny dots to us, because they are so far away, but most are actually extremely large.

What is space?

Beyond our world there are many other objects. Some are colorful and massive, others distant and mysterious, but all of them are moving. In between, there are enormous, empty gaps that we call space. We also use the word "space" to refer to everything that lies outside our own world.

IT'S QUIET UP THERE...

When something makes a sound, the noise spreads out into the air around our ears. Our world is full of air, which is why we can hear lots of sounds – but there is no air in space. Even if we could take an entire orchestra into space and sit next to it, we would not hear any of the music – not even the drums!

Our nearest neighbor

After the Sun has gone down, the Moon is the brightest thing in the sky. The Moon is the closest object to us in space, much closer to us than the Sun. Although it looks quite big in our sky, it is many times smaller than the Sun.

Up in space there
are gigantic areas
of nothingness.

Gazing at stars

We live on a planet, and
most of the bright dots in our
night sky are stars. The nearest star
to us is the big, yellow-orange ball we can see
during the day – the Sun. It is much bigger than a
planet like ours. The Sun looks enormous in our sky
because it is so much closer to us than other stars.

*This satellite
is an object
in space that
is lit up by light
from the Sun.*

Why is it so dark in space?

Light is something that travels through space. Day and night, all
the light we receive comes from the stars. We can only see light
when it hits an object and bounces off it. Our planet (Earth)
is nice and bright because light can bounce off tiny specks,
called "particles," in the atmosphere around it (see page 7).
Space is empty, so there are no particles for the light to hit.

There is a giant ball of
solid metal at the center
of our planet. This is the
Earth's "core."

Nearly three
quarters of the
Earth's surface is
covered in water.

Planet Earth turns and travels
in space, but here on the ground
we cannot feel it moving.

Earth spins around as
it travels. It takes just
under 23 hours and
56 minutes for it to
make one full turn.

Why is the sky blue?

Sunlight is made up of different colors. When the light reaches Earth
its different colors bounce off tiny particles of dust and water vapor in
the atmosphere. Because of this, the colors get scattered all around
in the sky. The blue parts of the light are scattered more than the
others, which is why our sky looks blue during the day.

Our place in space

Our home in space is called Earth. It is a planet, a huge world that moves around in space. Planet Earth is largely made of rock, but most of the surface is covered in water – our seas and oceans.

Lively planet

Earth is the only planet we know of where living things can survive. Many different kinds of plants and animals live on this planet – so many, in fact, that nobody has counted them all. Plants and animals need water and a gas called oxygen to live. There is plenty of both on planet Earth.

AN INVISIBLE FORCE

If somebody dropped an object, it would fall down toward their feet. This is because everything on Earth is held in place by a special, invisible force called gravity. Earth's gravity pulls everything down toward the ground – so without this force we would all float up into the sky, and our oceans would spill into space! Earth is not the only place in space where this force is at work – gravity exists everywhere in the universe.

Luckily, the conditions on Earth are just right for living things.

Special blanket

Our planet is covered in a thick layer of gases called the atmosphere. We cannot feel this layer, but it contains the air that we breathe and the clouds that give us rain. It is important because it lets in all the light and heat we need from the Sun, but keeps out all the harmful things in the Sun's rays. The outer part of our atmosphere is where Earth ends and space begins…

A closer look

It is easy for us to see familiar objects in the night sky, such as the stars – but space is a big place, so there is always more to discover. People practice astronomy to get a closer, clearer look at things in space, or simply to try to see as far away as possible. Exciting new finds are being made all the time.

The Great Bear

The Centaur

Space patterns

The first astronomers made patterns out of the stars in our sky – like connect-the-dot pictures – to help them tell the stars apart. These patterns are called constellations. Each one has its own name.

The astronomer's tool

There is a special instrument, called a telescope, which helps astronomers to see distant objects in space. It works like a very strong magnifying glass, making objects look much bigger and clearer to the eye. Telescopes come in different strengths and sizes.

The Hubble Space Telescope (HST)

The biggest and most powerful telescopes are kept in large buildings called observatories.

Eyes in the sky

Earth has a thick atmosphere, which gets in the way when astronomers are trying to see objects more clearly. To get a better view of things, some large telescopes are based high up on mountains – where the atmosphere is thinner and clearer – or even in space (on board specially made satellites).

WOODEN WONDERS

The first telescopes were made around 400 years ago. They were not as powerful and accurate as today's equipment, but helped astronomers to make important discoveries. In 1781, an English astronomer called William Herschel discovered the planet Uranus using a wooden telescope. Today, astronomers do not even have to look into the sky themselves, because their telescopes have special computers that can collect the information for them.

Radio telescopes

Some telescopes work by tuning in to radio waves from space. The large dish picks up the radio waves and focuses them onto the antenna, which then turns them into electrical signals. A computer uses these signals to build up pictures of objects in space.

Antenna

Dish

Journey to the Moon

Apart from planet Earth, the Moon is the only place in space where human beings have walked. There have been six successful missions to put people on the Moon, all between 1969 and 1972. A total of 12 astronauts have explored the surface.

Launch of the Saturn V *rocket, July 1969.*

Rocket ride

In 1969, three American astronauts set off from Earth in a space capsule called *Apollo 11*. The capsule was launched into space by *Saturn V*, a powerful rocket. In space, the *Apollo* craft separated from the rocket and made its way toward the Moon. When it reached the Moon, a special lunar landing module, called the *Eagle*, dropped down onto the surface with two astronauts inside.

This is what our planet looks like from the Moon.

A rocket journey to the Moon and back takes about six days.

A view seen by few

The crew of the *Apollo 8* spacecraft were the first people to see an "Earthrise" – Earth rising above the lunar landscape (above) – when they flew around the Moon in 1968. Earth's daytime side is lit up by the Sun, while its nighttime side is lost in darkness.

A special visor protects the astronaut's eyes from the Sun's bright rays.

Astronauts on the Moon can only talk to each other by using the special radios inside their helmets.

The backpack contains a supply of air.

With no wind to remove them, an astronaut's footprints could stay in the Moon's soil for millions of years.

Moon machine

The first men to walk on the Moon were Neil Armstrong and Edwin "Buzz" Aldrin. This is the *Eagle* craft which took them down onto the surface – and later, back to *Apollo*.

The lower part of the craft was left behind when the Eagle left the Moon.

Moon walking

The Moon's gravity is much weaker than Earth's. This means that objects on the Moon are not pulled down toward the ground as strongly. This makes walking difficult. In fact, the easiest way to get about is by hopping like a kangaroo! A Moon astronaut could jump almost six times as high as a person on Earth.

Armstrong and Aldrin spent nearly a whole day on the surface. Meanwhile, Michael Collins orbited the Moon inside the Apollo 11 *command module.*

Back with a splash

The *Apollo 11* command module, *Columbia*, made a safe return to Earth by falling into the Pacific Ocean. This is called a splashdown. After the module had come back into Earth's atmosphere, three parachutes opened out to slow it down on its way toward the ocean.

Earth's moon

The Moon is the largest, brightest object in our night sky. But, unlike the Sun, it has no light of its own to give out. It looks so bright because its surface is lit up by the Sun. There is no air, weather, or life of any kind on the Moon.

Moving around

The Moon is always traveling in space – on a path around our planet. This journey is called an orbit. As it travels, it also turns like a spinning top. It spins exactly once during each orbit of the Earth.

Our moon is like a nighttime lantern in the sky.

This is where the Eagle module landed.

Near side

These dark patches are called "seas," but they do not contain any water.

This picture of the Moon was taken by the Apollo 11 spacecraft as it flew back to Earth.

A secret side

The same side of the Moon faces our planet all the time. This means that there is one side that we can never see from Earth. The far side (right) is very different from the near side (left). There are fewer dark "seas" but many more craters.

Far side

When it faces the Sun, the Moon's rocky surface can get too scorching hot to touch.

Data zone

- The Moon travels around the Earth in just over 27 days.

- A Russian space probe called *Luna 3* was the first spacecraft to take pictures of the far side of the Moon.

These bowl-shaped hollows on the surface are called craters.

Very old ice

The *Lunar Prospector* space probe (above) discovered some frozen water near to the Moon's north and south poles. This ice is probably left over from comets that crashed into the Moon's surface a long time ago.

Does the Moon change shape?

As the Moon moves around the Earth, we see different amounts of its sunlit side. This is why the Moon seems to change shape. These changes are called the phases of the Moon. The first phase is the new moon, when it cannot be seen at all. Then we see the crescent, the first quarter, the gibbous, and finally the full moon.

New Moon   Crescent   First Quarter   Gibbous   Full Moon

The Sun

The Sun is the nearest star to Earth. Like all stars, it is an enormous ball of burning, scorching hot gas. It is a fiery monster, but the Sun is what makes all life on Earth possible.

This probe has been exploring the unknown regions of space above the Sun's north and south poles.

The *Ulysses* space probe

Fantastic fireworks

The Sun's center, or "core," is like an enormous furnace where gases burn. At the surface, gas leaps up in bright bursts called solar flares. Often, these blasts of really hot gas arch up high above the surface to form "solar prominences" – great big, fiery loops.

A loop-shaped prominence leaping out.

Sunset light show

It is dangerous to look directly into the Sun because it is so bright. One way of enjoying our local star more safely is by watching the sky at sunset. As the Sun sets, we can see more of the colors in its light – and the beautiful patterns they form.

14

Storms on the surface send "blastwaves" into space. These can damage satellites, and even cause power outages on Earth!

The center of the Sun is like a giant bomb that never stops exploding.

An eclipse of the Sun

A solar eclipse takes place when the Moon passes between the Sun and Earth. When this happens, the Moon stops some of the Sun's light from reaching us and casts a shadow on parts of our planet. At these places on Earth, day turns to night for a short time.

It takes eight minutes for the Sun's light to reach planet Earth.

Family of the Sun

The Sun is at the center of a neighborhood of planets called the solar system. Earth is one of nine planets that each make a special journey, called an orbit, around the Sun.

All the planets travel in the same direction around the Sun

Sun

Asteroid Belt

Jupiter

Mercury Venus Earth Mars

Jupiter takes nearly 12 Earth years to orbit the Sun.

The "inner planets" are made of rocks and metals

Sun and planets not to scale

Each planet spins on a tilt

16

Planets and moons

A moon is a large, rocky object in space that orbits a planet. Moons come in a variety of sizes, but most look like small planets. Apart from Mercury and Venus, all the planets have one or more moons. Saturn and Uranus have more than 20 each!

This is Callisto, Jupiter's second largest moon. It is the same size as planet Mercury.

...but at different speeds.

Saturn

Saturn has at least 22 moons, and astronomers are always looking for more.

Uranus

A Neptune year is the same as 165 Earth years.

Neptune

Pluto has the longest path around the Sun.

Pluto

...the "outer planets" are fat, gassy giants.

...but some tilt more than others.

SPINNING TOPS

All the planets spin, or "rotate," as they travel in their orbits around the Sun – but each one spins at a different speed. Even though it is the largest planet in the solar system, Jupiter turns the fastest. It makes one full rotation in less than 10 hours. Earth rotates once every 23.93 hours.

Hot planet, cold planet...

Mercury is scorching hot during the day, when temperatures are four or five times greater than the hottest places on Earth. But its thin atmosphere is not able to hold on to any heat from the Sun – so at night, Mercury quickly plunges into a deep freeze!

If people moved to Mercury, they would be four times as many years old!

Mercury and friends

Mercury, Venus, Earth, and Mars are known as the "inner planets" because they are the nearest to the Sun. These globes are made up of the same kind of materials – mainly rocks and metals – and have a solid outer surface called a crust.

Lonely explorer
The US *Mariner 10* probe is the only spacecraft ever to have visited Mercury. It set off in 1973 to help make a map of the planet's surface.

The days on Mars are almost the same length as those on Earth, but the seasons are twice as long.

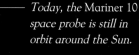

Today, the Mariner 10 *space probe is still in orbit around the Sun.*

Rivers once flowed on the surface of Mars.

Collision course
Mariner 10 discovered that Mercury is covered in large dents and hollows called craters. These were caused by rocky objects in space, called asteroids, which crashed into the surface of Mercury.

The Earth's atmosphere is thick enough to protect it from most asteroids.

Too hot for humans
Venus has a thick atmosphere that hides the surface from view. It works like an enormous winter blanket, trapping all the heat from the Sun. Because of this, Venus is the hottest planet in the solar system.

SPACE RACER
It takes just 88 Earth days for Mercury to complete its journey around the Sun – so it has the shortest year in the solar system. It is also the fastest-moving planet, which is how it got its name. In Roman mythology, "Mercury" was the name of the swift-footed messenger of the gods.

Sister Venus

Venus is the closest planet to Earth. Some call it our "twin sister," because it is almost the same size and is made up of the same kinds of rocks and metals as Earth. But it is not a good home for humans.

Poisonous planet

Venus has a cloudy, swirling atmosphere – like planet Earth has – but Venus's is burning hot and poisonous. The yellow clouds in the sky are full of a harmful acid. If it rained, it would burn our skin.

This picture of the landscape on Venus was made by a computer, using information from the Magellan spacecraft.

Stormy winds blow the clouds around the planet at high speeds.

There are no rivers, seas, or oceans on the surface of Venus.

Data zone

- Planet Venus is named after the Roman goddess of love.

- The sky is orange on this planet, and it is always cloudy.

- The atmosphere on Venus is like a pressure cooker. Visitors would shrivel up in seconds and roast like potatoes!

Bright as a star

Light from the Sun bounces off the thick clouds on Venus. So Venus often looks like a big, bright star in our sky just before sunrise and just after sunset. This is why astronomers call Venus the "morning" or "evening" star.

Venus (top middle) in Earth's evening sky

Spare parts in space!

A space probe called *Magellan* (right) has helped scientists to make a map of Venus's surface. This spacecraft is made out of leftover parts from the *Viking*, *Voyager*, *Galileo*, and *Ulysses* space probes.

Venus's rocky surface has been shaped by volcanic eruptions.

Ugly sister

The *Magellan* craft saw that Venus has lots of jagged mountains and monstrous volcanoes, just like on Earth. This volcano is one of the largest on the planet. Its name is Maat Mons.

THE LONGEST DAYS IN SPACE?

On Earth, there are 24 hours in a day and 365 days in a year. A Venus year is shorter than ours – 225 of our Earth days. But the really amazing thing about Venus is the length of its days, which last for 243 Earth days. This means that a Venus day is actually longer than a Venus year!

Martian volcanoes

The volcanoes on Mars are the giants of the planet. Olympus Mons (Mount Olympus) is the biggest volcano on Mars, and may even be the largest in the solar system. It is three times taller than Mount Everest, the largest mountain on Earth.

These dark circles are enormous volcanoes that can be seen from space.

This big split in the surface of the planet is a giant canyon called Valles Marineris.

On Mars, the dust storms can last for weeks.

Postcard from Mars

This picture was taken by *Pathfinder* – a spacecraft that landed on Mars in 1997. *Pathfinder* carried a small, robotic vehicle, called the *Sojourner* rover, which explored the surface and looked at Martian rocks.

The Red Planet

On clear nights, Mars is a bright, red disk in our sky. The rusty, red dust on its surface and in its atmosphere makes this planet look like a hot, dusty desert – but it is actually freezing cold.

Blue sky at night

When there is dust in the atmosphere, the daytime sky on Mars is a dusty pink color. As the Sun goes down, the sky just around it turns from pink to blue. If it is very dusty, the sky can glow for more than an hour after sunset.

This antenna sent out signals containing the information that the spacecraft collected.

Two special, moving cameras took the first clear pictures of the surface.

The weather monitor studied wind speed and temperature.

Vikings on Mars!

In 1976, two robotic spacecraft landed on Mars. *Viking 1* and *Viking 2* used mechanical arms to scoop up and test the soil, looked at the weather on Mars, and sent pictures of the surface back to Earth.

The robotic arm and scoop moved soil into the craft, where it was tested.

Potato moons

Phobos and Deimos are tiny, potato-shaped moons that orbit Mars. They are so small that they may once have been asteroids (space rocks) that were dragged into orbit around Mars by the planet's gravity. Mars has no other moons.

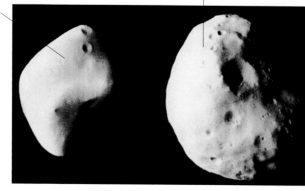

Deimos

Phobos

A rocky racetrack

In addition to planets and moons, there are millions of smaller, rocky objects in the solar system. These are called asteroids, and most travel together in the asteroid belt – a wide, circular track of rocks that are racing at different speeds around the Sun.

Roaming rocks

Not all space rocks live in the asteroid belt – some move around on their own. These asteroids can get pulled toward moons and planets by their stronger gravity. The smaller pieces of rock and dust that break off from asteroids and comets are called meteoroids.

Stony barrier

The asteroid belt lies between Mars and Jupiter. It is a little like a dividing wall between the smaller, "inner" planets and the big, gassy giants like Jupiter and Saturn.

The asteroids are "spare parts" – like building blocks that were left over when the moons and planets of the solar system were formed.

Data zone

● There are usually thousands of miles between the asteroids.

● Most meteoroids burn up completely when they get into Earth's atmosphere, but some large chunks manage to hit the ground from time to time. These are called meteorites.

● One asteroid, called Ida, is bigger than a city and has its own moon – named Dactyl.

What is a shooting star?

When meteoroids travel through the top of Earth's atmosphere they get very hot and burn up. This makes a long streak of light in the sky. These streaks are called meteors – but are also known as shooting stars.

The biggest asteroid in the belt, called Ceres, is the same size as France.

Many of the asteroids look like small space boulders, while others are enormous, rocky monsters!

DINOSAUR KILLER?

Many astronomers think that the death of the dinosaurs was caused by a mountain-sized asteroid that crashed into Central America 65 million years ago. This would have caused the planet to cool down, making it difficult for the dinosaurs to survive.

King of the planets

Jupiter is the largest planet in our solar system. It is so big that all the other planets could fit inside it. Bright red and yellow clouds drift around in Jupiter's atmosphere, making it one of the most colorful objects in space.

Gas giant

Jupiter belongs to a group called the "gas giants" – a family of planets that also includes Saturn, Uranus, and Neptune. The gas giants all have a hard center, but their top layers are made of gas – very different from Earth's rocky surface.

Jupiter has four very large moons – Ganymede, Callisto, Io, and Europa – and lots of smaller moons.

In ancient Roman stories, "Jupiter" was the name of the king of the gods.

A MOON WITH AN ICY SECRET

Europa is Jupiter's fourth largest moon. The surface of Europa is completely covered in smooth ice. Information from a spacecraft called *Galileo* has shown that there could be a layer of water beneath the ice. Some scientists think that the warmer parts of this secret ocean might be home to tiny forms of alien life.

Interesting Io

Io (pronounced "eye-oh") is a very strange place. It is covered in volcanoes that spit hot lava from the center of the moon out onto the freezing cold surface. Here, the lava cools down and turns into bright patches of solid rock. As this goes on, Io is actually turning itself inside out all the time!

Io is one of Jupiter's biggest moons. These bright yellow and orange splotches make its surface look like a giant pizza!

Great Ganymede

Ganymede is the largest moon in the solar system. It is bigger than the planets Mercury and Pluto. Because it travels around Jupiter, and does not orbit the Sun by itself, it cannot be called a planet.

Ganymede is made of a mixture of rock and ice.

Jupiter's Great Red Spot is three times wider than planet Earth.

The Great Red Spot

One of Jupiter's most familiar features is the giant red spot among its clouds. This is actually a dramatic storm, similar to an enormous hurricane, which has been rumbling on for over 300 years.

The probe fell for nearly an hour before it was crushed by Jupiter's atmosphere.

Brave explorer

The *Galileo* spacecraft arrived at Jupiter in 1995. The main craft circled the planet while a small probe dropped down into Jupiter's atmosphere. With a parachute to slow it down, the probe studied the atmosphere and used radio signals to send information back to the *Galileo* craft.

Squashed orange

Jupiter and Saturn are both large blobs in space that bulge in the middle. Saturn is the "flattest" planet in the solar system, and looks like it has a fat, hungry belly!

Saturn

Some of the bits and pieces in Saturn's rings are as small as sand grains and ice cubes. Others are as big as houses.

Most of Saturn's moons are just tiny, icy worlds.

Titan is the second largest moon in the solar system and looks like a small, mysterious planet. Its surface is hidden away under thick, orange clouds.

Playful moons

Like planets, Saturn's moons have their own gravity. As they travel around the planet in their orbits, the moons use this force to pull and tug at Saturn's rings. This pulling changes the way the rings are set out, and makes gaps in between them.

Planet Saturn has a squashed top and bottom.

Chilly Enceladus has a freezing cold surface that is completely covered in ice.

Mimas travels just outside the rings, and has a giant crater on its surface.

Titan

Rhea

Iapetus

Dione

Enceladus

Mimas

Planet of the rings

Saturn is a beautiful planet, best known for its colorful rings. It is the second biggest planet in our solar system – and has a large family of at least 22 moons. Before we had telescopes, Saturn was the most distant planet that astronomers knew about.

Voyage to the rings

In 1980, the *Voyager 1* spacecraft took a closer look at Titan, Saturn's largest moon. It also made important discoveries about the mysterious rings of Saturn.

A day on Saturn lasts just 10 hours and 40 minutes.

BIG SOFTY

Saturn is bigger and made out of more material than Earth, but this material is not so tightly packed together. The stuff that makes up Saturn is more spread out – this means it has a lower "density." If it was possible to drop all the planets into a gigantic bucket of water, Saturn would float. All the others would sink like stones.

Each ring is made up of hundreds of tiny ringlets.

This is a "false color" picture of Saturn's rings. The colors were added to show the differences in the rings.

Rings of light

Saturn's rings are made up of icy rocks of different shapes and sizes. The icy chunks and grains are like mirrors that reflect the light from the Sun. This is why the rings are so bright and dazzling.

Distant twins

Uranus and Neptune are "gas giants," like Jupiter and Saturn. These two planets look very similar and are made of the same materials. But like all brothers and sisters, their looks hide many differences…

Messy Miranda
One of Uranus's moons, Miranda, has a cluttered surface full of craters and icy cliffs. This moon may have been broken apart at one time, before its pieces settled back together again.

Tilts and turns
Like Earth, Neptune rotates on a slight tilt as it travels in space. Uranus moves differently – it lies entirely on its side, "rolling" like a wheel as it orbits the Sun.

Planet Uranus has 21 tiny, icy moons.

Planet Uranus is slightly bigger than Neptune.

Uranus and Neptune are lonely, chilly worlds.

Voyager 2 *has left Neptune. It is now traveling on a lonely journey out of our solar system...*

Bright white clouds drift around in Neptune's atmosphere.

Neptune is the windiest planet in the solar system.

Voyager 2 discovered 10 of Uranus's 21 moons.

On a voyage

After visiting Jupiter and Saturn, the *Voyager 2* space probe flew on to Uranus in 1986. The force of gravity then pulled it on toward Neptune, which it reached in 1989.

Neptune has at least four rings – but they are extremely faint. They are made up of very tiny, dustlike particles.

Far away worlds

Uranus and Neptune are the most distant of the four gas giants. It took eight and a half years for *Voyager 2* to reach Uranus. Neptune is even more remote – it is 30 times further away from the Sun than planet Earth.

Uranus has 11 narrow rings. The rocks in the rings are among the darkest in the solar system – a little like coal.

A LONG WAIT FOR SUMMER...

As Uranus rolls around the Sun on its side, one half of the planet receives light from the Sun all the time while the other half remains dark. Because of this, Uranus's north and south poles have 42 years of summer and 42 years of winter. If it were possible to live on Uranus, people would have to wait a very long time for a change of season.

31

Charon

Pluto

Dancing partners

Pluto has one moon, called Charon, which moves around Pluto every six days. As they move and turn, Pluto and Charon keep the same sides facing each other – like dancers twirling in space.

A PLANET, OR NOT A PLANET?

Some of the icy objects that orbit the Sun live in the Kuiper Belt. This is a huge ring of icy, cometlike objects which stretches from Neptune to the Oort Cloud. Some astronomers think that Pluto may actually be the largest of the objects in the Kuiper Belt, rather than a true planet. Even so, this chilly, distant world is still known as one of the planets.

Pluto and the comets

Pluto is the smallest planet we know – a lonely, freezing cold world of ice and rock. But is it *really* a planet? There are lots of other icy objects, such as comets, which move around our solar system. Pluto could be a long-lost relative of these icy travelers.

A year on Pluto lasts for 248 Earth years.

Pluto's orbit

Pluto's path
All the planets travel on orbits that are shaped like an ellipse (a stretched circle). Pluto's orbit is stretched and tilted the most. This means that its distance from the Sun also changes the most as it travels.

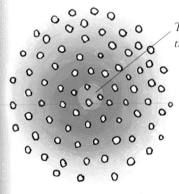

The Sun and the planets are at the center of the Oort Cloud.

Comets are made of rocky dust, snow, and ice. When close to the Sun, they have a thick dust tail (yellow or white) and a thinner gas tail (blue).

The Oort Cloud
Billions and billions of comets form a gigantic, ball-shaped place called the Oort Cloud. This stretches all the way around our solar system. Way beyond Pluto, the comets travel on vast orbits around the Sun.

Shape changers
Here on Earth, we can only see comets when they leave the Oort Cloud. As it journeys close to the Sun, a comet gets brighter and increases in size – growing a great big head and two long tails.

A star is born

Stars are made in swirling clouds
called nebulas. Nebulas are made
of gas and dust which bind together
to form gigantic, spinning balls.
These young stars quickly heat
up and shine, making the nebula
glow in beautiful colors.

Stars change as they grow
older, and eventually
they die – but only after
many billions of years.

Secrets of the stars

Stars are the true giants of space. They are the most common objects in the night sky, but in many ways the most complicated. Astronomers have spent years solving the mystery of how stars "live" and "die" in space.

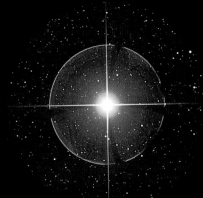

Supergiants and supernovas

The biggest stars, called supergiants, live for the shortest time. When supergiants run out of fuel they collapse in the middle, sending their outside layers into space with a gigantic, dazzling-bright explosion. This is called a supernova.

How do stars die?

Stars die when they have run out of fuel. Smaller and mid-sized stars, like our Sun, die very gently and quietly. They swell up to become a huge "red giant," and then slowly cool and shrink as layers of gas are pushed away into space.

WHAT IS A BLACK HOLE?

When a "supergiant" star ends its life in a supernova, the leftover parts and pieces usually form something called a neutron star. But sometimes, gravity pulls so hard on the leftovers that they all squash together and shrink into a single point in space. This is known as a black hole.

Star recycling

Stars begin their life as gas and dust wandering through space. Eventually, they become gas and dust all over again – but these materials will be "recycled" when they are used to form fresh, new stars.

The Milky Way

A galaxy is a huge family of stars that travels around in space. The Milky Way is the name of our galaxy, and it contains all the stars you can see in the night sky. Mixed in with the stars are enormous clouds of gas and dust. These bits and pieces are the building blocks for new stars.

Spiral galaxy

Barred spiral galaxy

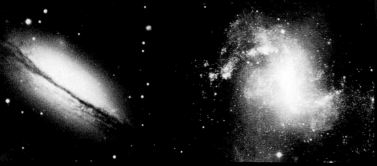

Elliptical galaxy

Irregular galaxy

Shapes in space

There are galaxies of different shapes and patterns, but they can be grouped into four main types – spiral, barred spiral, elliptical, and irregular galaxies. Like moons and planets, galaxies spin and move around in space. The Milky Way is a spiral galaxy.

The stars in the Milky Way travel around the center of the galaxy on these spiral arms – but they are not all moving at the same speed.

Although it is made up of millions and millions of stars, the Milky Way is mostly just empty space.

Pancake galaxy

The Milky Way is flat when seen from the side, but it has a large bulge at the center. Stars of different ages, sizes, and temperatures travel around the middle of the galaxy in enormous, sweeping bands called spiral arms.

The central bulge

Astronomers think that a great big black hole lurks at the heart of the Milky Way.

Data zone

● The shape of the Milky Way is always changing – but very slowly.

● Our solar system lies halfway along a busy spiral arm called the Orion Arm.

● It takes 220 million years for our solar system to go once around the center of the Milky Way.

A smudge like us

The Andromeda Galaxy is the furthest thing we can see from Earth using just our eyes. Although it is a gigantic mass of stars, to us it looks like a tiny blur in our northern sky. If we were able to look out from the Andromeda Galaxy, the Milky Way would also be nothing more than a bright smudge in space.

About the universe

The "universe" is everything that exists, including the things we cannot see and do not yet know about. It is hard to imagine just how enormous the universe is, because it seems to have no beginning and no end...

Galaxy watching

The *Hubble Space Telescope* is helping astronomers to make new discoveries about the universe. It focuses on tiny areas of space to produce pictures full of dots and smudges, like the one above. These pictures are of deep space, and the tiny specks are actually entire galaxies.

The Hubble Space Telescope *orbits Earth.*

Because of our swirling atmosphere, no telescope on Earth can see things as clearly as the Hubble.

Data zone

● Most astronomers now believe that the Big Bang was actually quite a small bang!

● Our solar system was not formed until millions and millions of years after the universe began.

To this day, we have only explored a very small part of the universe.

What is the universe made of?

Most of the universe is just empty space, but floating around in this space are galaxies like the Milky Way. These galaxies contain millions of stars of all different ages. Some of these stars have special families like our solar system.

GROWING AND GROWING...

Soon after the Big Bang, when the universe first began, all the things inside it were closer together – but as time has passed, these things have spread further and further apart. People have tried to guess the size of the universe, but nobody knows exactly how big it really is. However, astronomers have seen that the galaxies inside it are slowly moving away from each other. This must mean that the universe is getting bigger all the time.

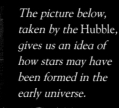

The picture below, taken by the Hubble, gives us an idea of how stars may have been formed in the early universe.

There are billions upon billions of galaxies in the universe.

Born with a bang!

Many scientists think the universe grew out of an explosion – known as the Big Bang – that happened many billions of years ago. They say that this explosion threw out hot materials which later formed all the galaxies, stars, moons, and planets in the universe.

39

Liftoff

One of the greatest challenges about space is getting there. To explore space, special vehicles have been built that are powerful enough to break away from the pull of Earth's gravity.

It takes just eight and a half minutes for a space shuttle to reach space.

All under control

There is a crew of astronauts on board every space shuttle flight – but their missions are directed from Earth. This happens at a place called Mission Control. Here, teams of about 20 flight controllers take turns keeping a close eye on the mission and study information sent back from the shuttle. This goes on all day and night.

A space shuttle orbiter can carry seven astronauts.

Testing laboratories can be set up inside the payload bay.

Delivery service

Space shuttles have a large storage area called a payload bay. It can be used to carry machines into space, such as satellites and space probes. The crew on board can visit the *International Space Station* (see page 43), repair satellites, and do experiments.

Looking down...

Satellites help us to learn more about Earth. Their pictures are used to make accurate maps of the surface. We can also forecast the weather using a satellite's view of cloud patterns.

Back in one piece

Rockets are launched much more frequently than shuttles and do various jobs, but they are not reusable. The US space shuttle is the only kind of spacecraft that can travel into space and back to Earth more than once.

The outside of the shuttle orbiter gets extremely hot when it reenters Earth's atmosphere.

Life in space

The very first people in space only went up in short "hops" to see what it was like. Today, astronauts can spend weeks or even months living and working in space, thanks to large satellites called space stations.

This picture was taken during a space shuttle mission to service the Hubble Space Telescope (right).

This robotic arm is part of the shuttle's Remote Manipulator System (RMS).

People grow about 2 in (5 cm) taller when they are in space.

Eating and drinking

Astronauts have a supply of specially prepared meals that they either heat up or add water to before eating. Some food and drinks are ready to consume right away.

Dried pear

Drinks

Meal tray (straps onto leg)

Weightlessness

Gravity is what makes us feel heavy, but astronauts on board spacecraft and space stations cannot feel it working on them. They feel weightless. People and objects that are not held down may float about inside the craft.

Beds on board

An astronaut's bed is a sleeping bag, with body straps to keep people from floating around as they rest. The crew always keeps the lights on, so eyeshades are also needed.

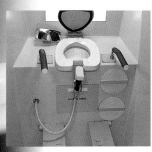

Hold on tight!

This is a suction toilet. It uses flowing air to suck the waste into a container. Users have to strap themselves in!

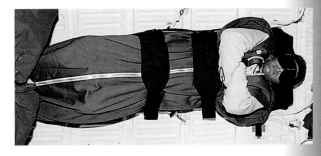

A man-made star

Sixteen countries are now working together to build the biggest ever space station. The *International Space Station* was started in 1998 and will take six years to complete. Its finished parts are taken into space by rockets and shuttles, where they are joined together by astronauts. When it is ready, it will be one of the brightest objects in the night sky.

Our future in space

One day, making a journey into space may be as familiar as traveling by airplane. Space agencies on Earth might even make it possible for ordinary people to take their first steps onto distant planets…

Data zone

● Astronomers have now found other planets beyond our solar system and are busy looking for more.

● In case they are found by alien beings, some space probes – like *Voyager 1* and *2* – carry special messages about our planet.

● Scientists have set up a base in the Arctic Circle to find out what it would be like to live on Mars.

Moon mining

In the future, it is possible that permanent bases will be set up on the Moon so that scientists can study it more closely. Robots may be used to begin the building work – using materials, such as iron and aluminum, that could be dug out of the Moon's surface.

A stepping-stone to Mars

If humans began to live on the Moon, in special moon bases, it might help us get to Mars. But even from the Moon, the trip to Mars and back would take a minimum of one year.

Expeditions to Mars may become possible later on this century.

Talking to aliens

This is the Arecibo Radio Telescope, which has the largest telescope dish in the world. Scientists have used this telescope to send a special radio message into space. They did this to try and make contact with alien beings.

Vacations in space

For years, people have been dreaming about going on vacation in space. Some day there may be hotels that drift in orbit around the Earth, with sight-seeing tours to the Moon.

Space glossary

This A-Z glossary contains the meanings of some words that are useful to know when reading or learning about space. All of the words are used in this book.

Air a mixture of gases that forms planet Earth's atmosphere.

Alien life living things on other worlds.

Asteroid a space rock.

Astronaut a human space traveler.

Atmosphere a layer of gases held in place around a moon or planet by its gravity.

Comet an object made of rocky dust, snow, and ice. Comets travel on very long orbits around the Sun.

Command module the part of the *Apollo* spacecraft that carried the astronauts to and from the Moon.

Constellation a pattern of stars visible in the night sky.

Core the stuff that makes up the center of a star, moon, or planet.

Crater a large, bowl-shaped dent in the surface of a moon or planet.

Crust the hard, rocky layer at the surface of a moon or planet. The inner planets all have a crust.

Density all things are made out of "stuff" (material). An object's density tells us how closely packed this stuff is. If something has a "high" density, its material will be tightly crammed together.

Gas giant a planet which has deep upper layers made mostly of liquids and gases.

Gravity the natural, invisible force of attraction between objects – such as the pull between Earth and the Moon.

Lunar this word is used to describe things to do with Earth's moon.

Martian a word used to describe things to do with the planet Mars.

Meteor the streak of light that is made by a meteoroid that travels through the top of a planet's atmosphere.

Meteorite a meteoroid that hits the surface of a moon or planet.

Meteoroid a piece of space rock that has broken off from a larger asteroid or comet.

Moon a natural object in space that travels (in orbit) around a planet.

Nebula a cloud of gas and dust in space where new stars are formed.

Observatory a large, dome-shaped building where very powerful telescopes are based.

Orbit the name for the journey that one object makes around another, bigger object in space. Things are held in orbit around other things because of gravity.

Oxygen the name of the gas that plants and animals on Earth need to survive.

Particle particles are the very tiny building blocks that make up all things.

Planet a large, ball-shaped object in space that orbits a star. The planets of our solar system orbit the Sun.

Planetary year the time it takes for a planet to complete one full orbit around its star.

Satellite any object in space that orbits another object. There are many man-made, or "artificial," satellites in orbit around Earth. Moons are "natural" satellites.

Shooting star another name for a meteor.

Solar a word used to describe things to do with the Sun.

Space capsule the section of a rocket where the astronauts travel.

Space probe a man-made spacecraft programmed to explore distant places in space.

Star stars (like the Sun) are extremely large, spinning balls of scorching hot, burning gas. They produce light and heat energy.

Useful websites

http://www.dustbunny.com/afk/index.html Astronomy for Kids!

http://www.the-cosmos.com/data/english/enhanced The Cosmos: a Search for Life.

http://www.discovery.com/guides/space/space.html Discovery.com Guides: Space.

http://www.exploratorium.edu/observatory/index.html The Exploratorium: Observatory.

http://hubble.stsci.edu The Hubble Space Telescope: HubbleSite.

http://www.pbs.org/deepspace Mysteries of Deep Space.

http://spaceflight.nasa.gov/index.html NASA: Human SpaceFlight website.

http://starchild.gsfc.nasa.gov NASA: "Star Child" astronomy site.

http://library.thinkquest.org/28327 A Virtual Journey into the Universe.

http://www.enchantedlearning.com/subjects/astronomy Enchanted Learning: Zoom Astronomy.

Index

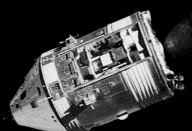

alien life, 26, 44

Andromeda Galaxy, 37

Asteroid Belt, 16, 24

asteroids, 16, 19, 23, 24-25

astronaut, 10-11, 40, 42-43

astronomy, 8-9

atmosphere, 7, 8, 19, 20, 23, 24, 25, 27

Big Bang, 38, 39

black hole, 35, 37

blue sky, 6

Callisto, 17, 26

Ceres, 25

Charon, 32

comet, 32, 33

constellation, 8

crater, 19

Daedalus, 15

day, 21, 29

Deimos, 23

dinosaurs, 25

Earth, 6-7, 10, 16, 17, 19

eclipse, 15

Europa, 26

galaxies, 36-37, 38, 39

Ganymede, 27

gas giant, 17, 26, 30, 31

gravity, 7, 11, 17, 35, 40, 43

Hubble Space Telescope, 8, 38, 42

Icarus, 15

International Space Station, 41, 43

Io, 27

Jupiter, 16, 17, 26-27

Kuiper Belt, 32

light, 5, 6

living things, 7

Mars, 16, 17, 19, 22-23, 44

Mercury, 16, 17, 18-19

meteorite, 24

meteoroid, 24, 25

Milky Way, 36-37, 39

Miranda, 30

Moon, 4, 10-13, 15, 44

moons, 17, 23, 26, 27, 28, 30, 31, 32

nebula, 34

Neptune, 17, 30-31, 32

neutron star, 35

Oort Cloud, 32, 33

orbit, 12, 16, 33

oxygen, 7

Phobos, 23

planets, 7, 16-17, 44

Pluto, 17, 32-33

radio telescope, 9, 44

red giant, 35

rings, 28, 29, 31

robots, 44

rockets, 10, 41, 43

rocks, asteroids, 24

satellite, 5, 8, 41

Saturn, 17, 28-29

shooting star, 25

sky, 6, 20, 23

solar system, 16-17

space shuttle, 40-41, 42, 43

stars, 5, 8, 14-15, 34-37, 39

Sun, 5, 14-17

supergiant, 35

supernova, 35

telescope, 8-9, 29, 38, 42, 44

Titan, 28, 29

universe, 38-39

Uranus, 9, 17, 30-31

Venus, 16, 17, 19, 20-21

volcanoes, 21, 22, 27

year, 16, 21, 33

Acknowledgments

Dorling Kindersley would like to thank: Hilary Bird for compiling the index, Emily Bolam for original artwork, and Andrew Nash for additional designs. Thanks, also, to the following DK staff: Elinor Greenwood and Penelope York for editorial assistance, and Diane Legrande (from the DK Picture Library), Lesley Grayson, and Bridget Tily for additional picture research.

Picture Credits:
(Key: a = above; b = below; c = center; l = left; r = right; t = top) Dorling Kindersley would like to thank the following for their kind permission to reproduce their photographs / images:

Anglo-Australian Observatory: 36cra, 36cbl, 36cbr. **European Space Agency:** 11cr. **Galaxy Picture Library:** Robin Scagell 8bl; 20cl; 21tl. **Genesis Space Photo Library:** 10cl, 43tl, 44cr. **NASA:** 2cla; 5bl; Finley Holiday Films 6c; 7b; 10-11; 11tl; 11br; 12c; 12b-13b; 13ca; 13br; 14cla; 15br; 16cl; 16-17c; 17tl; 18tl; 18tr; 19bl; Finley Holiday Films 19crb; 21cr; 22b; 22c; 22tl; 23cl; 24bl; 24-25c; 25tr; 26c; 27; 27cr; 27bl; 28c; 28b; Jet Propulsion Laboratory/Caltech 29cla; 29br; Finley Holiday Films 30tr; 30br; 31tl; 33br; COBE Project 37ra; 38b-39b; 38t-39t; 39cla; 39clb; 41tr; 41cla; 41clb; 42; 43cl; 43cr; 43br; 47tr. **NHPA:** Martin Harvey 7ca, 7tr. **NSSDC / GSFC / NASA:** 13cb. **Planet Earth Pictures:** Mike Read 4bc. **Powerstock Photolibrary / Zefa:** Stock Photos Pty Ltd. 14bl. **Royal Observatory, Edinburgh:** D. F. Malin/Anglo-Australian Observatory 34, 35crb. **Science Photo Library:** Dr. Seth Shostak 1; NASA 2l, 3r; Celestial Image Co. 4cl; Frank Zullo 4-5; David Nunuk 9; ESA/Photolibrary International 12tr; Pekka Parviainen 25tc; Lynette Cook 32; Royal Observatory, Edinburgh 35tr; Jean-Charles Cuillandre/Canada-France-Hawaii 36cla; Joe Tucciarone 36-37; NASA 40c; Allen Green 40bl; NASA 41bc; David Parker 44bc; Luke Dodd 46l, 47r; Celestial Image Co. 48l, 48r. **Shimizu Corporation:** 44tl, 45. **STScI / AURA / NASA:** B. Balick, J. Alexander/University of Washington 35cla. **Weatherstock:** Warren Faidley 6.
Jacket images: Front cover: NASA bc, cl, tr; NASA/Finley Holiday Films bl, br, c. Back cover: NASA/Finley Holiday Films c. Spine: NASA b.